SEMPER
OPERA HOUSE
DRESDEN
1985

SEMPER OPERA HOUSE DRESDEN 1985

VERLAG ZEIT IM BILD
DRESDEN 1985

February 13th, 1945–a historic date for Dresden.

Forty years ago in that night of horror on February 13th Dresden sank in ashes and rubble under the hail of bombs released by British and American bomber squadrons and, for a few moments, the breath of what was once the Florence on the Elbe, faded, although at that time the outcome of the Second World War had already been decided.

35,000 people killed, 75,000 homes completely destroyed and a further 100,000 damaged, 40 hospitals and clinics bombed–this is but a part of the havoc wrought by the more than 500,000 high-explosive and incendiary bombs dropped on the city.

Twenty-three churches and eight chapels were totally destroyed. Thirty-five schools and 68 cultural centres as well as eleven buildings of culturo-historical value–among them the Semper Opera House–were turned into ruins and heaps of rubble.

Did it really take place, that night of horror forty years ago? This is a question that is often posed by younger people as well as strangers to the city when they view the Dresden of today.

This speaks well for the city. It would, indeed, speak against the city and its inhabitants if they were to forget the fire storm that broke over them shortly after 10.00 p.m. on that February 13th, 1945. No–there can be no forgetting, and neither is there any intention of doing so.

February 13th, 1985–also a historic date.

Thanks to the Central Committee of the Socialist Unity Party of Germany and the Council of Ministers of the GDR another of the decisions taken at the Ninth Congress of the Socialist Unity Party has been translated into reality.

With great joy and expectation we, and with us thousands of people in our republic and abroad, have been looking forward to the completion of the historically true reconstruction of the Semper Opera House.

Part of the mission of the working class is the creation of new values while at the same time restoring and maintaining for our people those things from the past that are both valuable and humanist.

What began in 1945 with the rebuilding of the Zwinger has its continuation in the reconstruction of Gottfried Semper's world-renowned theatre building. It takes a worthy place in that ensemble of Dresden's most famous Baroque buildings which will be concluded with the reconstruction of Dresden Palace.

The opening of the Opera House is an event of historic importance for our city of music which is so rich in tradition.

When the curtain rises for Carl Maria von Weber's *Der Freischütz* at the opening premiere we take into commission a representative and modern theatre which has been rebuilt in its historic style, a theatre in which Dresden's operatic traditions will unite with the new, socialist music of today.

The "third" Semper Opera House, this historic, and at the same time, modern theatre building which takes its place among the best in the world, offers all the acoustic and technical conditions to make the realms of music available in the highest of quality to the broadest circles of the population, especially the working class.

The new Opera House provides testimony to the

far-sighted policy pursued by the working-class party and our socialist state as well as to the creative powers, the wealth of ideas and the assiduity of thousands of building workers, architects, engineers, conservators, restorers, sculptors and artists.

Both the leadership of the Socialist Unity Party and the government of the German Democratic Republic deserve our gratitude for their generous support in the realisation of this project.

Our greetings and thanks are also due to the builders who constructed the new building with so much devotion and personal commitment and in cooperation with the artists.

We wish to congratulate and thank all who gave of their best in the work of rebuilding the Semper Opera House: the bricklayers, the carpenters, the civil engineering workers, stuccoers, stone masons, painters, electricians, plumbers, locksmiths, all the planners and designers, the architects, restorers and visual artists as well as the workers from more than fifty factories, craft cooperatives and other enterprises and institutions in our country.

Complicated safety and clearing measures had to be carried through. Old foundations had to be demolished without causing damage to valuable substance still present. The often seemingly impossible was, however, achieved during the work of reconstruction.

A new supplementary building houses several rehearsal stages, dressing rooms and well-appointed social-welfare facilities; All this has vastly improved the working conditions of the actors and other staff members of the Dresden State Opera Company.

The opening of the new Opera House is an honour for Dresden's composers and musicians and places them under obligation to masterly achievements and performances in the cultivation and promotion of our cultural heritage, our socialist music culture as well as in the opening up of new works for the world's music culture.

May the unforgotten music of Carl Maria von Weber, Richard Wagner, Heinrich Schütz and other great masters, many of whom were once active in the city's opera house resound along with works by contemporary composers in the newly-built Opera House and bring joy, relaxation and assurance to its visitors.

I wish the people of Dresden and their guests impressive musical performances, an intellectual stimulus and pleasant hours of relaxation during their visits to the new Dresden Opera House.

Schill
Lord Mayor

OF MASTERLY DRESDEN OPERAS
AND OPERA HOUSE BUILDERS

Prelude

Dresden, the historic capital of Saxony, today the centre of a highly industrialised county in the GDR preserves manifold music and other traditions which date far back into the past. Hardly at any time previously, however, has the Dresden Opera Company, its origins and its continuity over a period of more than four centuries stood so much in the focus of international interest as it has during the eighties of the present century. The Semper theatre rebuilt by our society is now the attractive focal point, the centre of the architectural ensemble on Theaterplatz. But important anniversaries from the realms of operatic music form a no less festive moment in the socialist promotion of our heritage.

In 1983 such festive events were the 200th anniversary of the death of Johann Adolf Hasse and the centenary of the death of Richard Wagner. In 1985 we shall be honouring that great triumvirate Bach, Handel and Schütz, whereby it is particularly the 400th anniversary of the birth of Heinrich Schütz that draws the attention of the international music world to Dresden because the life work of this "father of the new music" is especially closely connected with the city of the River Elbe. And in 1986 we shall be celebrating the 200th anniversary of the birth of Carl Maria von Weber. As founder and music director of the "German Department" at the Royal Saxon Court Theatre from 1816 onwards

Weber laid the foundation stone for the introduction of a German national consciousness in the cultivation of the opera at the Court and with his *Freischütz*, which is set in the environs of Dresden, he took a decisive step towards a German national opera. His activities in the city initiated that period of development which reached its music theatrical zenith with the works of Richard Wagner in the 19th century and was carried over into the 20th century by Richard Strauss with his nine premieres in Dresden from 1901 *(Fire Famine)* until 1938 *(Daphne)*.

Counterpoint a cappella

Great anniversary celebrations of the past have already accustomed us to regarding that renowned document from September 22, 1548 in which the Elector Moritz of Saxony sets out the statutes of his *Cantorei* as the origin of an orchestra history in Dresden; further, this document is even extolled as being the "foundation charter" of the Dresden Staatskapelle orchestra. That is nowhere near correct. What was founded at that time was—when one excepts the organist—a community of singers, a choir. A look at the *Cantorei Statutes* shows that along with the first choirmaster, Johann Walter (a confidant of Martin Luther and recommended to the Saxon Elector by Philipp Melanchthon) we find ten adult singers, nine choirboys and an organist. The second *Cantorey Ordnung* from

1555 also underscored the clear precedence of the vocal art: seven "who are instrumentalists" the task of whom was to accompany the singers. The choir was responsible for arranging the court festivals, performing at meal times, taking part in the "inventions" and also singing for alms in the streets and squares. When looking at contemporary depictions one almost exclusively sees the singers in theatrically arranged scenes. When seeking the origins of Dresden's opera history one need not wait until the 17th century. The source of the city's promotion of opera is marked by just this *Cantorei* statute from 1548.

A distinction between *"Cantorey"* (choirmaster and singers) and the "instrumentalists" can be noted for the first time in the "Extract aus dem Hofbuch" in 1563. In the picture material that has been handed down, however, we can only see "Sagittarius" (the Archer), the previously mentioned "father of the new music", Heinrich Schütz (the word Schütze means archer in the German language) together with his singers in the old Dresden Palace choir. Indeed, in following the old tradition the choir boys belonged to the household of their choirmaster, this musical community was a family in itself.

De facto in the service of the Electorate of Saxony Heinrich Schütz revolutionised musical practice in the Electoral capital on the Elbe. In 1617, on the occasion of the centenary of Luther nailing his theses to the door of the Court Church at

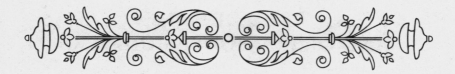

Wittenberg, he served his new Elector well: "The above music was festively rendered by the musicians ordered by the Elector of Saxony, namely 11 instrumentalists, 11 singers, 3 organists, 4 lutenists, 1 theorbist, 3 organ boys, 5 descant singers with the alternation of all sorts of fine instruments with two organs, 3 regals, 3 harpsichords along with 18 trumpets and 2 kettle drums under the direction of Heinrich Schütz from Weissenfels." Schütz had thus created an orchestra for his further activities in Dresden: from his choir of vocalists emerged a magnificent early Baroque orchestra which met the high artistic demands placed on it.

Overture

The genuine "birth certificate of the German opera" was made out by Heinrich Schütz, who had been appointed Director of Court Music to the Electorate of Saxony, some ten years later when Johann Georg I of Saxony led his daughter to the "royal consummation of her marriage" at Schloss Hartenfels near Torgau. Schütz had not only been commissioned to provide the musical background to the wedding festivities which were to last for a number of days, he was also expected to produce an especial attraction in the most modern form of art.
Schütz, who had studied the rapidly spreading musical-theatrical form of the opera in Italy itself, presented the first German opera with the ti-

tle *Daphne* in the dining hall of the Schloss on April 13, 1627.
"What Daphne gives is abiding," runs a passage in the libretto that Martin Opitz wrote, he was the author of the book "Von der deutschen Poeterey" and renowned as the "father of German poetry".
Actually in the title of the first German opera can be heard an early *leitmotiv* of Dresden's music history: the theme of Daphne accompanies us through Bontempi and Peranda's *Appollo and Daphne* (1671) in which, for the first time, a human being became an active antagonist in mythological-divine events right up to Richard Strauss' *Daphne* (1938) in which the huntsman Leucippus is set against the god, Appollo. But art and war exclude each other and a further *leitmotiv* contains a warning: Schütz's first German opera was written during the Thirty Years' War which devastated the whole of Central Europe between 1618 and 1648. Perceiving the horrors of this war with alert senses he made use of his art and continually repeated in his works his revulsion at the "loathsomeness of war", he bewailed the "wretched times" in which musical culture declines and is without means of livelihood; in 1636 full of grief at Germany he shed bitter "Tears of the Fatherland" in his *Musikalische Exequien*—after a decade previously his call to the warring princes (Da pacem Domini!) had gone unheard.
Three centuries later, in 1938, Strauss' *Daphne* was one of the last premieres before the outbreak of the Second World War which,

started by the fascists, brought death to millions and the destruction of the Florence on the Elbe and the Semper Opera House. When on February 13th, 1985 forty years after the destruction of Dresden by Anglo-American bombers, the doors of the Opera House open wide for all people of good will who are prepared to maintain this work of reconstruction, it will be our future concern to execute the testament of those great musicians which "hands down to our era the great traditions of the struggle for reason, liberty and humanity, for social progress and the 'harmony of the world'." (Theses for the Bach-Handel-Schütz Celebrations of the GDR in 1985) so that the words "What Daphne gives is abiding" may come to fulfilment.
"Fulfil her dreams,
Fulfil her love!
Undying
Evergreen
Let her prosper…"
(From: *Daphne*, 1938)

First Act

At the beginning of the 17th century opera and ballet performances were held in the halls, palais, pavilions or gardens of the royal court; the big festivals and "inventions" were held on public squares or in front of the (at that time still wooden) theatrical facade of the Zwinger. After the Peace of Westphalia (1648) had tamed the furies of war for the time being and new cultural activities could bestir them-

selves in Saxony, David Schirmer's ballet in verse *Paris and Helena* (produced for the first time in the royal palace in 1650) introduced a short flourishing period for the German-language music theatre, following the example given by Schütz. But Johann Georg II thought more of the Italian genre and thus Bontempi/Peranda's *Il Paride*, which was already played in 1662, is the first full opera performed in Dresden which has remained extant. But just how much even the Italians were captivated by the old master of German music is shown by their *Daphne* of 1671, based on the libretto by Opitz and the first German-language opera which is extant. The premiere of this work was celebrated in Dresden's first opera house that was built by Wolf Kaspar von Klengel on Taschenberg hill between 1664 and 1667. Not far from the Palace and connected with it by means of a passage the building done in sandstone from Pirna was one of the first theatre buildings to the North of the Alps and was extolled as one of the most beautiful, purposeful and biggest (it accommodated 2,000 spectators) opera houses in Europa. The building had been erected on a traditional place—from 1596 a ballroom had stood here at the south-west corner of the Palace "for the holding of festivities of all kinds".
Just how Klengel understood the art of theatre building may be gauged from the following Italian praise: "The Comedy House ... with its marble arches, columns and balconies could not be more magnificent

than it is and there is probably no other building of such beauty and quality in Europe." (G. Leti). After the opening with Moneglia's *Il Teseo* the Italians also dominated on this stage later on.
Saxony's grasp for the Polish crown brought new war and misery at the turn of the century, the country was bled white in the Great Northern War and art was once again without any means of livelihood. The musicians and other artists left Dresden and in 1708 the opera house was

converted into the Catholic Court Church as a result of Augustus the Strong's politically motivated embracement of the Catholic religion. Later it served as a ballroom, in 1804 it was converted to the State Archives and in 1888 it was demolished.
During the era of Augustus the Strong, both the Italian and the French influence dominated in the arts. Central theatrical events were the court festivals originating from the Renaissance traditions which

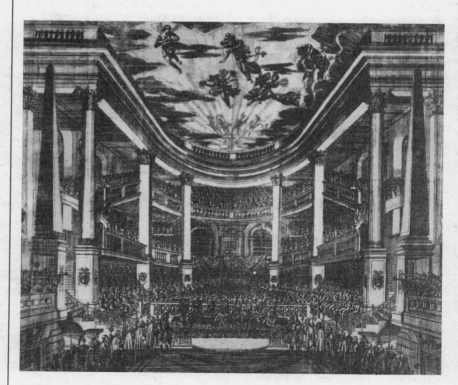

Auditorium of the Opera House on Taschenberg hill (1667–1690).

incorporated opera, ballet and other musical performances in a rich artistic totality of architecture, poetry, music and representation. Along with eminent instrumentalists from the Court Orchestra outstanding singers made the city extremely interesting for Handel, Telemann and Bach. This art epoch reached its climax with the marriage celebrations of 1719: these celebrations were the reason for rebuilding the Giant Hall in the Palace and for building the Grand Opera House at the Zwinger (in approximately the south-west corner of the present Zwinger—between the entrance to the Porcelain Collection and Postplatz).

The foundation stone was laid on September 9th, 1718, and on August 25th, 1719 the building was completed: the interior architects were the Mauro brothers whilst Pöppelmann was responsible for matching the facade with the architecture of the Zwinger. The Grand Opera House opened on September 3rd, 1719 with a performance of Lotti's *Giove in Argo*. With its interior dimensions of 24 × 54 metres the building was internally larger than the Church of the Cross; it was Germany's largest theatre and also one of the largest in Europe. The September celebrations had attracted visitors to Dresden from all over Europe and they had carried the fame of the sumptuous opera festivals celebrated by the Saxon Court out into the whole of the world. Particularly the stage, for the magnificent arrangement of which Giuseppe Galli Bibiena had been engaged, outshone everything hith-

erto. In contrast to other courts Augustus the Strong was interested in impressing the whole of the Dresden populace with his festivals. Although in the case of festive performances the theatre, which also seated 2,000 people, was reserved for the court society, in general criers announced the opera to be performed in the city and in the case of normal performances "Burghers and wives from the city" were allowed to take a seat in the upper circle.

In 1734 the epoch of Johann Adolf Hasse who, with his wife, the singer Faustina Bordoni, gave his first guest performance in Dresden in 1731, began in this theatre. As the

"uncrowned German king of Italian opera" he gave, along with his work together with the orchestra, the opera a Venetian atmosphere. Like Schütz, Hasse, too, devoted nearly all of his life's work to Dresden and took the magnificence of Baroque opera to its extreme: for the premiere of his *Ezio* (1755) 400 people, 102 horses, 5 carts, 8 mules and 8 camels were on the stage which was open as far as the Zwinger courtyard...

In 1745 as Frederick the Great, King of Prussia, moved into Dresden after the Battle of Kesselsdorf, he wrote, fascinated, to his valet Fredersdorf: "I cannot come to Berlin at once, I should also like to

Interior of the Grand Opera House (1717–1849).

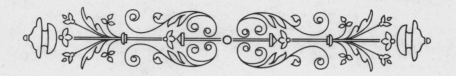

bring peace with me. Today *Arminius* is being played here, and there is music or opera almost every day." (*Arminius* was the Hasse opera premiered in 1745).

Although the thunder of this war had no deep-going effect on the Saxon capital the beginning of the Seven Years' War put a sudden end to the promotion of the arts in Dresden. Hasse's *Olimpiade* (1756) was the last big operatic event. In 1760 the Prussian king bombarded the city with his cannon and destroyed the greater part of its art treasures. The Opera House was badly damaged and later served the Prussian troops as a magazine. The valuable scores (the greater part of Hasse's scores and Schütz's manuscripts) were burnt during the bombardment. Even though the Grand Opera House at the Zwinger was provisionally repaired after the Peace of Hubertusburg (February 15th, 1763) and a further Hasse opera *(Siroe)* played on August 3rd, 1763, the death of Augustus III on October 5th, 1763 brought the Augustian era to an end. The Italian ballet and opera companies were disbanded, Hasse left Dresden with Faustina, the glorious days of the Baroque opera were irrevocably finished. A late afterglow of fame for the theatre came when the opera house was used for the marriage celebrations of the Elector Frederick Augustus III in 1769 and Johann Gottlieb Naumann's *La Clemenza di Tito* was performed. After the fourth performance of this opera the house was shut; it later served as a ballroom, was festively

illuminated when Napoleon entered the city in 1812 and came to late fame when it became the venue of the State Orchestra's subscription concerts. Particularly famous are the Palm Sunday concerts of 1843 when Felix Mendelssohn Bartholdy conducted his *St. Paul* and those of 1846 with Ludwig van Beethoven's *Ninth Symphony*, the rediscovery of which had been initiated by Richard Wagner. This latter concert marked the beginning of an unrenounceable line of tradition for the Dresden Staatskapelle. During the revolutionary days of May 1849 a fire razed the building to its foundations after which it was demolished.

Intermezzo popular

Although till now it is mostly the large representative theatres maintained by the Court which have been written about, the fact cannot be disregarded that there were already extremely interesting and, above all, popular episodes around the middle of the 18th century. An important new accent in Dresden's theatrical life was set by the Italian impressario, Pietro Mingotti, who came to the Saxon capital with an artistically well-trained opera company and requested a licence to build a theatre. The Venetian was permitted to build a small wooden theatre in the Zwinger courtyard (in front of the Wall Pavilion). This building was opened on July 7th, 1746 with the opera *Argenide* by Paolo Scalabrini, the conductor of

Mingotti's company. In a very short space of time its more popular repertoire made it a serious competitor for the adjacent Grand Opera House. This, of course, it was not able to do with operatic magnificence à la Hasse. Mingotti put his faith in the cheerful *opera buffa*, presented *pasticcios* (made up of excerpts from popular operas), and had with his wife Regina Mingotti, a prima donna with no less virtuosity than Faustina Hasse in the Grand Opera House. In 1747 she was feted in Pillnitz when Gluck's festive opera *Le nozze d'Ercole e d'Ebe* was performed under his own direction (Christoph Willibald Gluck was a member of Mingotti's company, as assistant conductor). "Through the neglect of a singer..." the theatre was burnt down in 1748 and this short intermezzo came to an end. But the need for a popular small opera house had been so greatly promoted that in the following period opera ensembles like Locatelli's also played in the Brühl Theatre (on Brühl Terrace approximately above the present "Bärenzwinger" Technical University Student's Club near the Albertinum). In 1754/55 another Italian impressario, Pietro Moretti, built a small wooden theatre near the Zwinger wall on the site of today's Theaterplatz square. After many architectural alterations this building, which initially accommodated 350 spectators, eventually developed into the Small Court Theatre (so named to distinguish it from the Grand Opera House at the Zwinger) where, subsidised by the Court, the most im-

portant European theatrical companies performed, companies like those of Bustelli, Bondoni, Seconda and Seyler. As from the beginning of the 1770s the Grand Opera House fell unused into disrepair and an increasing number of full operas were also presented at this Small Court Theatre. The premiere of Mozart's *The Seraglio* was held here in 1785 and in 1794 an Italian(!) *Magic Flute* was produced. Francesco Paer, Francesco Morlacci, for a short time E.T.A. Hoffmann, and lastly Carl Maria von Weber were all active in this theatre. It remained for Weber, on the basis of the stormy political changes that followed the liberation wars of 1812/13, with his *Freischütz*, composed in Dresden, to create the German national opera as such. That Richard Wagner as a child heard the *Freischütz* played in this theatre under the direction of Weber himself and that it had a great influence on him is something that should also be mentioned.

Of no less importance for the cultural history of Dresden's opera is the Summer Theatre at Linckesche Bad situated on the outskirts of the city towards Bautzen that was used from 1776 onwards.

During the winter months, and especially during the carnival season, the people of Dresden had their opera in the city, in the Small Court Theatre. During the summer months they went to Lincke where the same musicians and singers, etc., the troupe headed by J. Seconda, for example, presented both good and entertaining productions.

The Small Court Theatre (opened in 1755).

The Theatre on Linckesche Bad (opened in 1776).

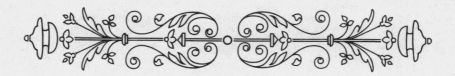

Music played by the municipal pipers in the garden, the sale of coffee and other beverages were, however, merely the trimmings to what were, in their own manner, demanding artistic experiences. This was the main place of activity for E.T.A. Hoffmann during his Dresden period; Beethoven's *Fidelio*, Weber's *Silvana* and Mozart's operas were played to a broad public here. The singer Wilhelmine Schröder-Devrient gave her Dresden debut here. It was in this suburban theatre that the new trends of a bourgeois opera culture won through in Dresden. Artistic competition may well have played a part—but it was, nevertheless, almost merely an act of administration when, in 1816, Count Vitzthum, the General Director of the Court Theatre, took the Theatre on the Linckesche Bad on lease and dissolved the Seconda company. The Court ran the Summer Theatre as secondary theatre until 1858.

It is thanks to Carl Maria von Weber, appointed to the office of Director of the Dresden Opera Company by Count Vitzthum on January 17th, 1817, that the various influences of national opera cultures from that time on united in their various characteristics and were able to function together as an entity...

Although he may not have experienced such grandiose premieres here as, for instance, Wagner later did with his *Rienzi, The Flying Dutchman* and *Tannhäuser,* Dresden did, nevertheless, offer Weber all those traditions which he needed as the source for his creativity.

Second Act

The dilapidated main building of the Small Court Theatre became more and more of an anachronism–the people of Dresden gave it the rather affectionate, if somewhat critical, epithet of "the mouldy pie". The time had come for something new in the city centre. In the bulletin issued by the provincial Diet it was stated that "the building bearing the name of the Royal Court Theatre is a genuine disgrace to the surrounding area and, indeed, to the city itself." Gottfried Semper was commissioned to build a new theatre and put forward his grandiose "Forum Plan" which–taking up ideas mooted in the Augustian epoch–was to continue the Zwinger enclosure right down to the banks of the River Elbe. But despite the enormous growth of the Saxon capital, the population of which increased from 51,175 in 1813 to 63,886 in 1830 and to 94,092 in 1849, it was only the new Court Theatre that was built–the grand new city centre remained but a dream.

The new theatre was opened on April 12th, 1841. Suddenly the Dresden Opera House, which after the death of Weber, had been managed by Marschner and Reissiger, stood once again at the centre of interest for all Europe after this epochal architectural accomplishment. A massive sandstone building reflecting the semi-circular auditorium in its facade, the tasteful exterior of which incorporated early Italian Renaissance forms. This famous circular building of Semper's which at that time was known as the "most beautiful theatre in the world" was burnt out in 1869 as a result of one of the staff working carelessly in the attic above the chandelier.

Even though this epoch is today mostly closely linked with the name of Richard Wagner, the fact cannot be overlooked that–apart from *Rienzi*–his works were not particularly popular with the public. *The Flying Dutchman* had only four performances, *Tannhäuser* found no sympathy, the finale of first act of *Lohengrin* presented at the festive concert given on September 22, 1848 was a flop whereas Reissiger's contribution had to be repeated... What remained was nothing but a torso.

The defeat of the 1848/49 revolution was equivalent to the decapitation of the arts: the singer Schröder-Devrient, the conductor and revolutionary writer August Roeckel, the architect Gottfried Semper and with him many of Dresden's intellectuals had to leave the city just like Richard Wagner who was under warrant of arrest. In the decades between the *Tannhäuser* premiere in 1845 and Ernst von Schuch's taking office as Director of Music in 1872 only a few opera premieres enlivened the Dresden scene and Schuch, too, would need decades to make visible the fact that the hidden forces were nevertheless still effective and that they could not only be followed up but also continued.

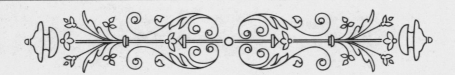

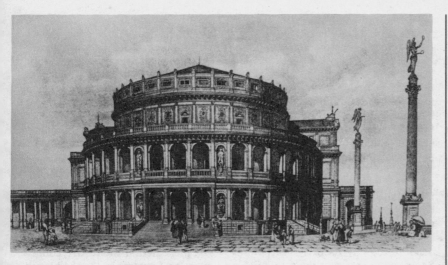

Semper's design for the first Court Theatre (1841–1869).

The provisional theatre (1869–1878).

Third Act

Following the fire in the first Semper building a provisional theatre in the Zwinger grounds, the so-called "wooden hut", was played in from 1869 until 1878. Built within the space of six weeks this building had four circles and seated 1,800 people. Here Ernst von Schuch appeared for the first time as conductor of the Italian Opera Company Pollini (with Padilla and Désirée Artôt). The young hothead was immediately engaged as successor to Karl Krebs who was going into retirement and as from 1872 he was mainly responsible for what happened in the world of music in the Saxon capital. With the laying of the foundation stone at the northeastern corner of the exedra the construction of the second Semper building began on April 26th, 1871, it was that new house in which the "Schuch era" once again brought Dresden international prestige. With a performance of the *Freischütz* the provisional theatre was closed on January 31st, 1878 and the second Semper theatre opened on February 2nd, 1878. Also serving drama until the end of the century, the new Court Theatre became purely an opera house following the building of the Albert Theatre (1873) and the Playhouse at the Zwinger (1911). With an exemplary company of singers, and aginst the wishes of the Court, Schuch finally brought success to Wagner's works and devoted himself to the new operatic works–irrespective of whether they came from Italy (Verdi, Puc-

cini, Mascagni), from the Slav area (Dvorák, Smetena, Paderewski, Rubinstein) or, like the first opera by Richard Strauss, from the German traditions.

After the death of Schuch in 1914 Fritz Reiner took his office and in 1922 Fritz Busch became manager of the opera company and General Director of Music. He continued the Strauss tradition initiated by Schuch and also deliberately promoted new operatic and concert works (Busoni, Weill, Hindemith, Schoeck, Wagner-Regény, Büttner). Under his leadership Dresden remained one of the most prominent opera cities in the whole of the world and became one of the main pillars of a German Verdi revival, a further number of Puccini's works were gained for the repertoire, and the house achieved historical fame with Russian works *(Khovanshchina* and *Boris Godunov).*

After the fascists had taken over power Fritz Busch was driven out of Dresden during a performance of *Rigoletto,* following a scandal arranged by the nazis. In protest Al-

Semper's second Opera House (opened in 1878).

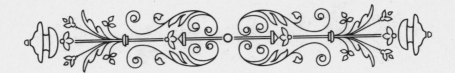

fred Reucker relinquished his post as general manager.

Between 1934 and 1943 Karl Böhm maintained the the artistic standards of the opera and even under the conditions imposed by the fascist regime was able to keep up the musical standards set by Schuch and Busch. Produced despite official opposition Strauss' *Schweigsame Frau* (1935), his *Daphne* (1938) and finally the premiere of his *Capriccio* in 1943 round off half a century the main characteristic of which is the abundance of the everlasting.

The Semper Opera House closed its doors on August 31st, 1944 after the proclamation of "total war" by the fascist regime. And total, too, was the destruction of Dresden: together with the enormous loss of human life, the whole of the city nucleus and all the theatre buildings in the city sank in rubble and ashes.

Coda–Oh, nameless joy

Thanks to the initiative and help of the Soviet Military Administration Dresden's first provisional theatre opened with a performance of Mozart's *Figaro* only a few weeks after the liberation from fascism. In 1947 the Saxon Provincial Diet renamed the Dresden Ensemble the "Dresden State Theatre/Dresden State Orchestra" and a year later the Grosse Haus (Grand House) of the Dresden State Theatre was opened to the public. Who, at that time, could not feel the significance of the moment when Christel Goltz– our greatest Leonore, Salome and

Antigonae of the post-war years– intoned "Oh, nameless joy" in the production of *Fidelio* presented on the opening night, September 22nd, 1948.

The pent up demand of the public which had been intellectually starved as a result of fascism and the war may initially oriented itself on recovering the classical repertoire. Those who were responsible for Dresden's opera, however, acted correctly when they permitted this demand to be fulfilled without dismissing the duties placed on them by tradition. Had they permitted all that which has been built up through the generations and which is firmly embedded in the public to come to an end we of today would not be in a position to work so comprehensively and assuredly with new works. With Blacher, Hindemith, Orff, Prokofiev and Karl Amadeus Hartmann it was not just any old "moderns" who were in the repertoire during those early years, but opera composers who showed the way for the new beginning, who were symbols of an artistic coming to grips with the most recent past. Dresden Opera came to be particularly proud of the fact that it was able to draw attention to GDR composers not a few of whom are citizens of our city: Otto Reinhold, Fidelio F. Finke, Karl-Rudi Griesbach, Karl Friedrich, Rainer Kunad, Udo Zimmermann...

With the laying of the foundation stone for the reconstruction of Semper's opera house the biggest task to be undertaken since its destruction in 1945 had been assigned. A con-

cept had to be found which drew on the historic heritage of a Schütz, Hasse, Weber, Wagner or a Strauss and which allied itself ever closer with all that is new.

All our activities live from the close community of public and artist–the critical assessment of what has been achieved and the discussion about what is to be achieved. The new building, the "third" Semper Opera House, places the highest of demands on both public and producers. Out of destruction, privation, struggle and accomplishment, work of reconstruction and success consciously achieved, a new theatre building, more beautiful than ever before, had grown up under the conditions prevailing in our socialist society.

It is the task of the building workers, the cultural workers and the whole of the population of our country to maintain this world-famous opera house for the generations to come.

THE RECONSTRUCTION OF THE SEMPER OPERA HOUSE DRESDEN

Theaterplatz square in Dresden, one of Europe's most eminent town-planning ensembles, lay in ruins at the end of the Second World War. In four day and night air raids between February 13th and 15th, 1945 British and American bombers dropped a total of 3,749 tonnes of bombs on the city killing 35,000 people. One third of all the homes and cultural centres were destroyed or seriously damaged— among them was the Semper Opera House. The outer walls, burnt-out vestibules and foyers were all that remained of the building. Semper's legacy, to newly order German theatre building according to content and form, had been destroyed.

A decision adopted by the Ninth Congress of the Socialist Unity Party of Germany in 1976 and by the Council of Ministers of the GDR decreed the reconstruction of this, the most important theatre in our country; Semper's second opera house was to become the "third" Semper Opera House.

A large number of residential areas had systematically come into being in and around Dresden. The housing projects Prager Strasse, Seevorstadt East and West as well as Prohlis and later Gorbitz have provided many of Dresden's citizens with homes. The building workers fulfilled the high targets set by the Eighth Congress of the Socialist Unity Party of Germany. "Today Dresden is again a beautiful city that is cherished by its inhabitants and whose charm attracts hundreds of thousands of visitors from all parts of the GDR and abroad year

18

The photo of the model for the reconstruction of the Semper Opera House in Dresden shows the separation of the theatre building from the functional building. The rehearsal stage is on the Elbe side and the restaurant is on the Zwinger side (page 17).

for year. The creation of new values whilst at the same time restoring and maintaning for our people those things from the past that are valuable and humanist—all this is part of the mission of the working class. What began with the reconstruction of the Zwinger we are continuing today by newly creating the Semper Opera House in its old beauty. We can hardly honour the memory of that great architect and revolutionary democrat Gottfried Semper in a better manner..."
(Erich Honecker, General Secretary of the Central Committee of the Socialist Unity Party of Germany and Chairman of the GDR State Council, 1977).

With the reconstruction of the Semper Opera House parallel to the *Neue Gewandhaus* concert hall in Leipzig; the building of the new *Friedrichstadtpalast* variety theatre; the reconstruction of the *Deutsche Theater* and also the reconstruction of the *Schauspielhaus*, built by Karl Friedrich Schinkel, in Berlin, significant impulses were imparted to the fields of cultural and music creation for maintaining progressive traditions through the means of art, for the increasing of the national culture and placing it in the service of peace. Fully aware of their great responsibility the collective of building workers, restorers and artists took up this unique, noble and difficult task.

The first protective measures were carried through on the ruin in the 1950s; the auditorium and the stage house were roofed in and the facades restored. At the same time

preliminary examinations were made so that exact building plans could be drawn up. The point of departure was the enlargement of the building planned by Wilhelm Kreis in 1938. The functional demands of theatre building in the 19th century are difficult to bring into harmony with today's theatrical practice. The search for the best solution was passionate and characterised by a high scientific content. At the end of 1975 the designing collective headed by Chief Architect Hänsch put forward a solution representing a functional entity which, however, strictly separated the historical from the new. The reconstruction of the whole of the building in its spatial structure, the original décor and colouring meets with Semper's demand that the functions of a building must be expressed in its ground plan, outer construction and ornamentation. The necessary ancillary functional buildings fit in with the Semper Opera House itself and, from a town-planning point of view, form no less interesting areas alongside the Zwinger Park and the former Bellevue Hotel that was destroyed during the war. Contact between the buildings themselves has been minimised and self-supporting connecting passages like those already existing between the *Schloss* and the Cathedral or the *Schloss* and the *Taschebergpalais* guarantee the functional relationship.

The enterprise *VEB (B) Gesellschaftsbau Dresden* was nominated as General Contractor for the Reconstruction of the Semper Opera House in 1974. Its sphere of competence

After the senseless air raid the Opera House was nothing but a chaotic heap of stone and steel. The stage-house walls stretched skywards; the auditorium was burnt out; the roof, balconies and stalls were completely destroyed; the brickwork had been cracked by the pressure; the steel girders had been deformed by the heat.

Lord Mayor Gerhard Schill is given the cassette to be laid in the foundation stone on the "Day of the Building Workers of the GDR" on June 24th, 1977. This was the symbolic start of the reconstruction of the Semper Opera House.

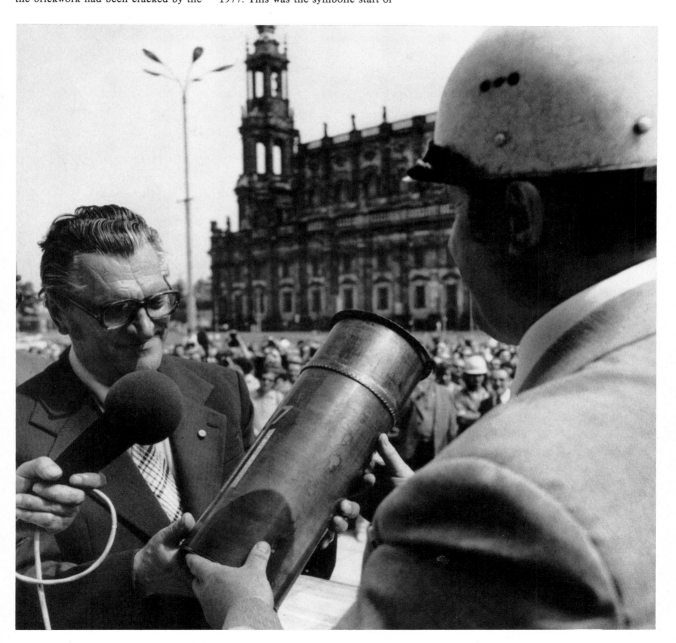

22

covered both design and the realisation of all reconstruction operations. Working in close cooperation with the *Bauakademie der DDR*, the *Institut für Denkmalpflege*, the *Institut für Kulturbauten DDR, Berlin,* Dresden Technical University as well as a number of specialised design institutes, the design division of *VEB (B) Gesellschaftsbau Dresden* worked out a project that could be carried through.

It was possible to retain to a great extent the exterior and the interior of the Semper building in the forms dictated by the Italian High Renaissance. As the seats of the fifth balcony and the proscenium were no longer available because of the installation of the lighting equipment, the floor space of the auditorium was enlarged to achieve a seating capacity of 1,284 in the stalls and balconies with standing room for 39 people in the fourth balcony. As the outer walls of the auditorium could not be altered, the cloakrooms for the audience were placed below the storey containing the stalls. A repetion of the unfavourable view of the stage and the uncomfortable, cramped arrangement of the seating in the auditorium was avoided by arranging the stalls more steeply and increasing the number of rows in the balconies. The partitions between the boxes have been cut back to a minimum of architectural necessity. Using material from the archives of the *Dresden Institut für Denkmalpflege* the ornamentation for the auditorium was designed on the drawing board by a collective of interior de-

corators headed by Zimmermann in order to restore the historical architectural motifs and festive decorational details to the central section of the theatre.

At this stage of the work particular attention had to be paid to the room acoustics as new conditions had arisen because of the changes that had been made in the geometry of the auditorium. Dresden Technical University carried out acoustics tests on a 1:20 scale model: the results of these tests conformed with the parameters of the orginal building.

The spatial structures of the vestibules and foyers were retained. The restorers removed the few still remaining traces of the burnt colours from the 1912 repainting and laid free the original colouring of the dome cap, the coffer-work, the ceiling lunettes and the wall ornamentation of 1878. An enlargement and thus change of shape in the stage area could not be avoided. The latest advances in theatre technology and modern technical equipment called for the addition of side stages to the former main and back stages. The necessary conditions for this were provided by accommodating the actors' changing rooms in the functional building, designed by Löschau and calculated as a project by *VEB Kombinatsbetrieb Forschung und Projektierung Dresden* attached to *BMK Kohle und Energie Dresden,* and by moving out the badly damaged outer walls of the stage building a distance of six metres.

In the designing and installation of the stage machinery the General

Although some demolition work was necessary, the work of reconstruction pressed ahead. Site managers, foremen, and work brigade leaders made sure that the drawing were kept to. Complicated foundation work had to be carried out. Surveys in the stage house showed that considerable underpinning of the foundation was necessary. The foregoing protection of various sections of the building called for great skill and experience on the part on those responsible. The pits for the side stages were prepared.

24 The three medallions in the exedra– Apollo, three Graces and Marsyas– were not fully destroyed but a restoration was indispensable. Helmar Helas completed the representation of Apollo after comprehensive drawn studies (left). The lunettes of the Upper Vestibule depict landscapes as the venue of famous dramas. There were but few remains for reconstruction. Restorer Liebscher examining what had been found (right). Many public figures who had been connected with Dresden's operatic life in former times informed themselves about the reconstruction work. Chief Architect Hänsch explaining the concept to the conductor Professor Karl Böhm who, shortly before his death, conducted Schubert's Symphony in C Major in the city. Plan discussion with Director

Tempel at "VEB (B) Gesellschaftsbau Dresden"–the search for better and quicker ways of working was permanently on the agenda.

Gottfried Semper's plan for the construction of the theatre placed, following the imperial Roman sovereign emblem, the richly decorated and coloured exedra in front of the circle formed by the Upper and Lower Foy-

ers. The badly damaged exedra was reconstructed by restorer Hennig.

26 Four artists worked on the decorative curtain of the Opera House. After the reconstruction undertaken by Helas—the draft design made by Professor Ferdinand Keller of Karlsruhr in 1875 was available—Franz Tippel painted the middle section "Fantasy with the torch of rapture". Dr. Siegfried Wunderlich undertook the work on the frieze of the poets and composers as well as the representation of the genii. Bernd Böhm and Michael Münch, proven theatre painters, executed the ornamental paintings.

The reconstruction of the 19-metre-long proscenium frieze was in the hands of Gerhard Keil and Walter Teichert. Matthias Schulz, head artist, and Werner Haupt, from the "Canaletto" Cooperative, checked the affixing of the canvas in the Opera House.

Günther Thiele was responsible for the decorative forms of the column shafts. Schulz, Kloss and Friedemann modelled the figures for the proscenium walls as well as the decorative elements on the balcony facings. All models were mounted in situ by stuc-

coer brigades Richter and Röbisch from "VEB Ausbau".

28 Certain sections of the cellar had to be deepened before the understage machinery was installed. The work was hampered by the high ground water level. This work was done by collectives from "VEB Bau- und Montagekombinat Kohle und Energie Hoyerswerda, Kombinatsbetrieb Industriebau Dresden", and "VEB (B) Gesellschaftsbau Dresden". The technologies were developed by the engineers Pilz and Büchner. Under the direction of foreman Lehmann workers put up the shuttering boards for the concrete work of the central cloakroom.

The transport of all building material to the auditorium cellar, later the large air-conditioning centre, went through the stage house. Every ten days a balcony segment in three sections was formed in the auditorium. The ceiling of the air-conditioning centre was closed with reinforced precast concrete sections at a later date. In part the collectives under Project Manager Dietze worked in a two-shift system, an important precondition for an early start to the stucco work on the balcony facings the walls of the auditorium and the ceiling.

30 The steel roof construction (with a total weight of 180 tonnes) was placed in position by the constructional workers from "VEB Sächsischer Brücken- und Stahlhochbau". The outer walls of the side stages consisted of sandstone and bricks. 100 years later the building workers mounted precast reinforced concrete supports and locking sections. The roofing was done simultaneously with the construction of the outer walls—a method that saved both material and time. The carpenters and concrete workers of "VEB (B) Gesellschaftsbau" worked alongside the stuccoers from "VEB Ausbau" in a race for time. In the building schedule all activities were technologically coordinated and a time lag could not be permitted.

The construction of the balconies presented many a complicated problem for Project Manager Nitschner and his men. From a structural point a view the construction of the four balconies in three segments should have been carried out in a diagonal sequence.

The reinforced concrete supporting plate of the balcony, the auditorium enclosing walls and the ceiling of the gallery were framed-in on the interior of the historic enclosing wall and cast in one process. "VEB Kartographie und Geodäsie" carried out all the

measuring and surveying work for this project.

From 1978 on six tinsmiths from "VEB Technische Gebäudeausrüstung Dresden" executed the large-scale roofing work on all the roofs of the Semper Opera House and the functional building.

Contractor was supported by *VEB Sächsischer Brücken- und Stahlhochbau Dresden* for the steel and technical constructions; *VEB Starkstromanlagenbau Leipzig/Halle* for the electro-technical work; and *VEB ORSTA-Hydraulik* for the hydraulic equipment. Apart from the rigid steel construction of the main stage (area 30 × 22 metres) with 16 hydraulic lifting stages in chess-board formation (each stage is 16 sq. metres in area) the understage machinery consists of two sides stages (each 17 × 25 metres) with three side stage carriages (4 × 6 metres) and an enlarged backstage (18.5 × 18.5 metres) including a backstage carriage (16 × 17 metres), and a rotating stage (15.5 metres in diameter). The orchestra pit is fitted with a lifting platform. The stage house is 34 metres high from the stage floor to the roof ridge and it has a depth of 10.5 metres from the stage to the cellar floor.

The portal opening is 11 metres high and 15 metres wide. The upper machinery consists of the portal unit itself with a two-deck lighting bridge and two portal towers each 18 metres high with 6 platforms, a double horizontal lighting bridge, 45 machine stage prop hoists (for the first time fitted with an electronic height indicator), two point hoists, three lighting hoists, three backcloth raising units for the fire and decorative curtains, a two-piece main curtain, noise and gauze curtains and three steel closure curtains to the back stage.

A machine-powered transport system in the stage house is duplicated in the scenery magazine and greatly facilitates the transport of set decorations to and from the stage.

The new theatre workshops near the Zwinger in Julian-Grimau-Allee, incorporate the former royal stable with its Classicist indoor riding hall and the "Ausspanne" hostelry. The three-storey terminal building contains the tailors' shop, the shoemakers' shop, the milliners' studio and various other rooms. The scenery painting hall (54 × 22 metres) and the workshop building with wood and metalworking facilities are adjacent. The building, designed by Dr. Pfau, Gustavs and Werner, is set together from precast sections and was awarded the Dresden County Architectural Prize in 1982 as well as the prize of the journal *Architektur der DDR* in 1983.

On the opening of the second Dresden Court Theatre in 1878 the architectural historian Richard Stecher wrote: "The colouring of the Dresden theatre is a masterpiece of the first order, an incomparable triumph of art. May it be protected." This obligation was broken twice. The repainting undertaken by Goller in 1912 as well as the total destruction of the iconography and the colouring on February 13th, 1945 set the art historians, restorers and conservators a great, and more than difficult, task. As a result of the disregard paid the architectural achievements of the 19th century, the painting cycles and statues had never been systematically documented. In 1979 Dr. Magirius, the Chief Conservator of the *Dresden Institut für Denkmal-*

Site manager Frank from "VEB SBS" was in charge of preparatory work for the fitting of the supports for the 500 tonnes of sandstone walling above the opening for the side stages. The civil engineering calculations were carried out by Engineer Thiele from the design division of "VEB (B) Gesellschaftsbau Dresden". The steel constructional workers operated at a height of 33 metres above the cellar floor of the auditorium. The roof trusses were fitted together on Theaterplatz. A "Gottwald" crane lifted the elements to the required height and set them on the outer walls of the building. The roof is formed by reinforced concrete slabs set on purlins.

34 The west facade is surmounted by an allegoric figural group "Love and Justice"–the models of the sandstone figures were created by Werner and Christian Hempel from photographs. Below the sandstone acroteria six masks after themes of the ancient theatre have been let into the facade. The head of Gottfried Semper is represented below the coat of arms. This sandstone work was executed by Emanuel Semper, the brother of the project-managing architect Manfred Semper. The backstage is situated in front of the functional building and the rehearsal stage. The masks on the rehearsal stage building were created by P. Makolies.

The exedra building is crowned by the panther quadriga with Dionysus and Ariadne, the work of Johannes Schilling. This bronze statue survived in the original. The head of Pan, a sandstone decoration on the socle of the quadriga (right). Stonemasons from "VEB Elbenaturstein Dresden" completed the facade. For this, old and lost skills such as rustication had to be re-learned.

36 The main stage consists of 16 lifting stages. Günter Schapke from "VEB Sächsischer Brücken- und Stahlhochbau" was responsible for the stage design work. The individual units can be hydraulically operated from −2.5 metres to +2.5 metres, the floor can be tilted to a maximum of 12 per cent. At rest it can carry 8 tonnes, on the move 4 tonnes. The first stage was demonstrated to the reconstruction management board and the experiences gathered used for the whole stage. The guiding elements were then completed.

Gottfried Ringelmann, complex site manager from the general contractor, "VEB (B) Gesellschaftsbau Dresden", and his deputy, Christian Teschke, visited "their" work collectives every day for situation reports and management decisions. Along with the precision work called for in lifting in the 4-metre high supporting beams for the side stage openings (above right) "VEB SBS" did high quality work in the designing, construction and fitting of the backstage carriage. The steel under construction of the rotating stage weighs 34 tonnes: electric motors raise or lower it at a speed of 0.5 metres/second and turn it at a speed of 1 metre/second.

pflege found, after a systematic search, the 109-page *Album des Kunstfonds*. This and the result of archeological examinations of the colouring in the vestibules and foyers beneath the burnt oil paints of 1912 as well as the first tests for the reconstruction of Semper's colouring in the left-hand part of the Upper Circular Foyer (1969/70) provided the foundation for the artistic design of the auditorium. Together with free-lance artists, the "Canaletto" painters' and decorators' cooperative was assigned the task of carrying through the painting and decoration work. Satisfactory results were obtained after a two-year period. After the complicated work of removing the colours the preparation of the undercoats, the colour layers and the tracing-on of the ornaments produced by artists in the original size could begin. Along with the gilding, a task consuming much material and time, in various techniques the members of the "Canaletto" cooperative also carried out the typical artisan painting and decoration work in the whole of the Opera House.

In the meantime a studio for the production of the large ceiling paintings in the auditorium had been set up in the Palais in the Great Garden. Many of James Marshall's large proscenium and four oval ceiling pictures by Keil, Teichert and Schietzelt; Theodor Grosse's eight oval ceiling pictures for the Upper Circular Foyer by Pukall; the lunettes of the Upper Vestibule by Symmangk, Rosenlöcher, Schreiber, Kecke, Hoffmann, Pietsch, Decker

and others were all painted here. Paul Kiesling's cavetto paintings in the exedra were executed *in situ* by Frau Böhner and Hennig under the direction of Helas after whose death the art management was taken over by Schulz. The sculptors found themselves a place to work near the stucco workshop. Here capitals, friezes, column bases as well as the proscenium statues were reconstructed from photos or the small pieces that had survived the air raids. Landgraf, Neubert, Schulze and Thiele are names representative of the many. The statues and objects on show in all the rooms, be it figural decoration or bands of fruit, were manufactured by stuccoers from *VEB Ausbau* in a workshop specially installed for the purpose.

In 1979 the *Institut für Leichtbau* manufactured three functional models of the historic lamps for the trial transverse axis of the Upper Circular Foyer. After this phase Brettschneider made all the patterns for the brass castings. From 1978, and in cooperation with *VEB Formguss Radeberg* all the necessary castings, from preliminary to final models, for the individual pieces with a total weight of 1.9 tonnes were manufactured. For the large chandelier this foundry alone delivered 1,440 ornamental castings, chased after founding, to *Spezialleuchtenbau Wurzen*. From 1980 on girdlers, metal formers, form-turners and sheet metal workers produced 363 lustres, wall and ceiling lamps true to the originals in brass. All the pressed parts for the lustres were manufac-

Engineer Hans-Joachim Bauer, director of "VEB (B) Gesellschaftsbau Dresden", thanked everybody for the work they had done and, as General Contractor, announced that the collectives had pledged themselves to keep all future schedules. Decorating the topping-out wreath with sprigs of fir and colourful ribbons were a sign for many of Dresden's citizens that the building work would soon come to an end. The last stage of the work of reconstruction of the Semper Opera House began for the builders.

40   In the auditorium the stuccoers from "VEB Ausbau" worked on the balcony facings. The bottom steel structures were mounted on the reinforced concrete supporting plates. After the stucco had been applied the outer form of the balcony geometry had been created. The mussel-shaped stucco elements on the balconies affect, according to Semper, the acoustics. Twenty-eight matt green column shafts in the side vestibules were made of artificial marble. Careful rubbing-down and polishing have given their surfaces a wonderful lustre. The half columns of the Upper Circular Foyer are fluted and were manufactured in the same manner.

Many long-forgotten craft trades and working methods had to be relearned. The decorative painting, including that of the figures, began at an early stage in the left vestibule. The view from the stage into the finished auditorium gives an idea of the effect on the audience. The fifth balcony has been fitted out as lighting gallery (p. 42/43).

Members of the "Canaletto" cooperative worked together on the painting of the severies of the side vestibules. Although the impression given by the vault painting by W. A. Schaberschul is one of richness there are only four motifs which, however, are distributed

tured from 0.6 to 1.5 mm thick sheet metal that was manually formed on wooden mouldings by means of steel rollers and forming tools. Form-turners carried out precision-turned metal parts from rods and cast parts. After surface treatment—grinding, polishing, burnishing and lacquering—the lustres were assembled.

The large chandelier in the auditorium is five metres high and 4.20 metres in diameter. All the brass parts are affixed with screws. The chandelier has 258 electric bulbs. The opal flashed glass was provided by *VEB Vereinigte Beleuchtungsglaswerke Dresden*. Complicated milling work on the square tubes was carried out by the *Institut für Leichtbau Dresden*.

The old Semper Opera House already had a ventilation system for the auditorium and foyers, this, however, did not meet up to the demands of the present day. The system had a steam-driven ventilator with rivetted vanes and a leather-belt transmission. Today the theatre building has 27, the functional building 12, the theatre restaurant 8 and the theatre workshops 9 ventilating units.

The two main units in the theatre building itself supply 712 people in the stalls and 611 in the balconies with conditioned air. The power-saving system of micro-conditioning ensures comfort: pressurised and undercooled air reaches the seat backs via the pedestal, where it is blended with sucked-in room air and blown out through the upper edge of the arm rest.

New, too, is the air-conditioning in the stage house. Intimate theatre must be air-conditioned just as large scenes with choir. The air-conditioning plant is variable from full to $1/3$ capacity. The control panel and central cold air plant are accommodated in the functional building. The refrigeration plant for cooling the air operates with heat pumps which heat the water for the sanitary installations and the air-conditioning plant. *VEB Lufttechnische Anlagen Dresden* was in charge of all this work from designing to installation.

VEB Nachrichtenanlagenbau Dresden installed comprehensive electro-technical systems. These serve the production of modern musical works. The electro-acoustic aids enable modern stage technology to be used to the full. There is, for instance, the playing of echo and other sound effects as well as recorded music. Close cooperation between the interior decorators and the designers of the electro-acoustic plant made masterly solutions possible. Sound dispensers in the auditorium are situated in the stalls and behind the lamps in the balcony facings. Seventy-seven loudspeakers alone were mounted in the ornamental painting on the ceiling.

By including the foyers, vestibules, cloakrooms and the cellar restaurant in the communications system, it is possible to indicate the beginning of the performance or the end of an intermission with a musical call-sign instead of the conventional bell. The electrical fitter Korbin was responsible for the laying

in such a manner that they do not repeat themselves in the neighbouring section. The white capitals show a sparing use of gold. After the columns and vaulting had been completed, the historic flooring of red terrazzo with light-coloured friezes was renewed or completed. Experienced specialists affixed the oval ceiling pictures in the auditorium into the painted frames.

46   Semper Opera House Dresden
Ground plan—stalls

Theatre building
1. Auditorium
2. Sound and lighting
control room
3. Orchestra pit
4. Gallery

5. Main stage
6. Back stage
7. Side stage
Functional building
1. Soloist dressing rooms
2. Ballet dressing rooms

3. Make-up room
4. Rehearsal rooms
5. Connecting bridges
Rehearsal stage

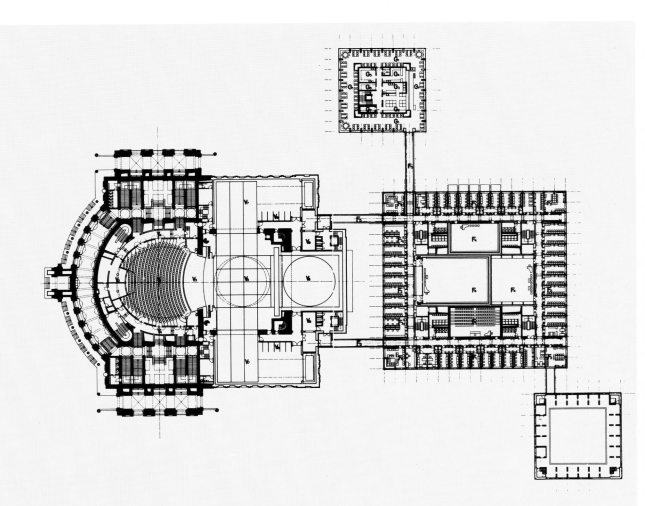

1. Dining room
2. Kitchen
3. Food preparing room
4. Washing-up area
5.–8. Storerooms

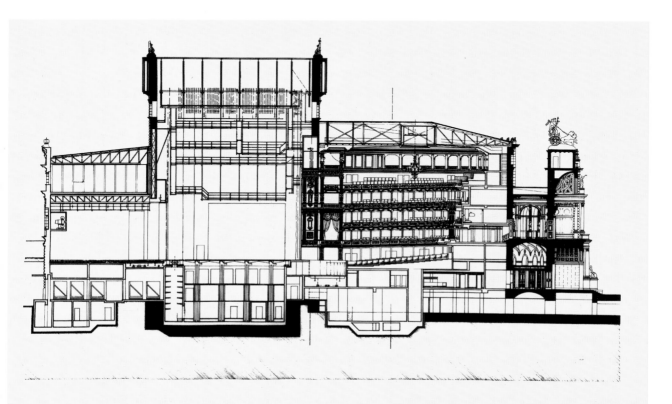

More than 1,858 constructional drawings had to be made for the theatre building to ensure that building operations ran to schedule. In the many special areas the work was coordinated in comradely cooperation. Certain technical equipment was not in serial production and had to be specially designed first. Among other items this applied to the electronic height indicators, the emergency lighting system, the balcony maintenance scaffolds, special spotlights, changeover switch gear for multiple mains connections, as well as to things like the supports for the stage towers, under-pinning technologies and special foundations.

48 The alarm system for the fire fighting equipment in the theatre and the functional building with rehearsal stage was installed by "VEB (B) Heizungs- und Sanitärtechnik". The project, which was designed by Müller and Schnelle from "VEB (B) Gesellschaftsbau Dresden" in cooperation with "VEB Elektroanlagen Ostsachsen" and "VEB Nachrichtenanlagenbau Dresden", envisages that in case of a sudden rise in temperature, a thermoindicator, and in the case of flue gas development, an ionisation indicator, trigger-off in the fire alarm centre the automatic or manual opening of the 19 sprinkler units for the affected section. The work was coordinated by Project Manager Böhnert.

A fitter from "VEB Elektroanlagen Ostsachsen" checking the functioning of the switching cell of the 20-kV installation. The electrical engineers Ander and Seyffert coordinated the work on this project. The cold water batteries from "VEB Maschinenfabrik Halle" are part of the air-conditioning plant (above right). An important component in all the 47 air-conditioning and ventilation systems is the KB 21–25 conditioning block from "VEB LTA Dresden" (below left). "VEB Heizungs- und Sanitärtechnik" installed the converter station in the functional building. From here a regulated heating medium is available for room heating, air conditioning and the piped hot water system.

The organ made by "VEB Jehmlich Orgelbau Dresden" is mobile and can be used for concerts or opera performances. It has 28 registers with 2,010 pipes on two manuals and pedals. All the historic outer and inner doors, wall panelling, cupboards and furni-

of 170 kilometres of cable in the theatre building; these cables connect the play-in studio, the sound studio, the stage manager's control desk, the two-way communication system, the radio staff and equipment locator system as well as the internal TV circuit. The rebuilt 5-minute clock in the auditorium is also connected with the centrally-controlled clock system. A wireless hearing system will make it possible for some visitors to better enjoy the musical experience.

The electro-technical equipment in the theatre building, the functional building and the theatre workshops as well as all the lighting in front of and behind the stage was installed by *VEB Elektro-Anlagenbau Ostsachsen Zittau*. Ten transformers ensure a constant voltage; the power needs of the whole theatre complex can be compared with those of a small town. 275 kilometres of cable and wiring are connected with 230 switch and distribution boxes. *VEB Starkstrom-Anlagenbau Leipzig/Halle* was responsible for the installation of the stage lighting equipment.

On June 24th, 1977 the foundation-stone was ceremoniously laid with the enthusiastic participation of the building workers and the citizens of Dresden. In the previous weeks complicated demolition and protective measures had been carried out on the ruins. The necessary building-site installations on Theaterplatz were installed by the bricklayer and carpenter work brigades of *VEB (B) Gesellschaftsbau* under site manager Ringelmann. Schoolchildren painted colourful pictures

on the wooden fence surrounding the site. *VEB (B) Verkehrs- und Tiefbaukombinat Dresden* were called on to undertake large-scale civil engineering work such as relaying the primary district heating lines and the water mains. A large number of wells were needed to sink the groundwater level. To protect the remaining cellar rooms of the old Semper Opera House it was necessary to sink five bore wells 16 metres deep in the immediate vicinity of the theatre building; these serve to feed off the water when the Elbe is in flood. To prevent danger to the functional building through backwater from the Elbe in flood the rainwater disposal system was redirected into the Zwinger pond. Twelve stonemason's shelters were set up for *VEB Elbenaturstein Dresden* with its "Sigmund Jähn" youth work brigade. Between 1977 and 1982 all ashlars, and richly profiled socles, pedestals, copes and balusters were restored or newly made and prepared for building in here. 1,400 cubic metres of manually worked ashlar from the *Steintagebau Mühlleite* near Lohmen; 400 cubic metres of machine-worked Cotta Sandstone ashlars from *Steintagebau Lohmgrund* near Pirna and 100 cubic metres of machine-worked ashlars with light-coloured Lusatian granite facings were moved by the Ripp work brigade from *VEB (B) Gesellschaftsbau*. The restoring as well as the new manufacture of the damaged and destroyed fine-membered statues in Elbe sandstone called for a high degree of intuition on the part of the stone masons.

ture were manufactured by "VEB Deutsche Werkstätten Hellerau". After the strip parquetry had been laid, fitters from "VEB Sitzmöbelwerke Waldheim" erected the chair frames. The seating in the stalls and the balconies was connected to the air-conditioning system within a few weeks. The seats in the stalls have red plush and those in the balconies green. The rows are 930 mm apart and the seats have a width of 550 mm.

52 Model sculptor Brettschneider from "WBK Dresden" formed the historic details of the big chandelier in full size. "VEB Spezialleuchtenbau Wurzen" and it partners manufactured in brass more than 2,000 individual pieces and mounted them. The richly decorated lamp consists of chased and polished brass pieces, as well as pressed and turned pieces. "Institute für Leichtbau Dresden" developed a special device for maintenance work on the lamps.

The outside diameter of the chandelier is 4.20 metres, the visible height 5 metres. The opal flashed silicate glass for the white globes was provided by "VEB Vereinigte Beleuchtungsglaswerke Dresden". The internal steel construction was delivered by "VEB Sächsischer Brücken- und Stahlhochbau" It has a total weight of 1.9 tonnes and can be mechanically raised or lowered. During opera performances the chandelier is not drawn into the ceiling of the auditorium.

The play-in studio can be used during performances and also for communicating with all stage areas. The five-minute clock, first built by Court Constructor Gutkäs was destroyed in 1869 during the fire in the first Opera

The *Verkehrs- und Tiefbaukombinat* needed 1,530 square metres of small cobblestone paving and granite slabs to pave the roads and the square.

The first phase of the building schedule was the securing and reconstruction of the walls and ceilings of the foyers and vestibules. The stuccoers from *VEB Ausbau* attached to *Wohnungsbaukombinat Dresden* started manufacturing the cornices, profiles and capitals—work calling for a high degree of skill—at an early date; in the course of six years the members of the Richter work brigade processed about 1,500 tonnes of plaster of Paris, 1,500 cubic metres of mortar and various other stucco materials.

All those walls and ceilings in the auditorium that no longer had a load-carrying capacity as well as those which disturbed spatial effects were removed by the Reinhard and Lehmann work brigades together with *VEB Autobahnbaukombinat.* The new geometric forms of the balcony area, designed by Hallbauer and John, were achieved through the use of reinforced concrete and it was not long before the stuccoers moved in and primed the material for Semper's colour composition of light sea-green broken with white and the sparse use of gold. The ceiling, balcony facings and proscenium were, in their essentials, finished in 1982 and the scaffolding was taken down on March 1st, 1983. For the first time the workers could see their work as a whole. Without any loss of time the floorers started to lay the par-

quet flooring so that *VEB Innenprojekt Leipzig Sitzmöbelwerk Waldheim* and *VEB Deutsche Werkstätten Hellerau* could begin with the seating. Special attention had to be paid to the stage house tower. The large breakthroughs in the outer walls for the side stages as well as the effects of fire on the sandstone walls had endangered its stability. 1,400 tension anchors as specified by the designers Kriesche and Thiele now join the two reinforced concrete shells around the weakened walls. Stabilisation measures were also necessary in the foundation level.

The topping-out wreath was hoisted in September 1981. The cooper roof had been completed; the men working together with Master Roofer Döschner from *VEB Technische Gebäudeausrüstung Dresden* had used sixty tonnes of sheet copper. *VEB (B) Heizungs- und Sanitärtechnik Dresden* installed the winter heating of the theatre building at an early date so that, as from 1977, the stuccoers, painters and other artists and craftsmen could systematically countinue their work. Work brigade leader Petzold and his men had already fitted the automatic sprinkler systems in the stage house and the rehearsal stage as well as the last sanitary installations while the Kappler, Richter and Kögler brigades were working on the air-conditioning plant and the power converter station.

The results of the acoustics tests from March 26th to March 28th, 1984 were awaited with great suspense. The building could be handed over. Following the com-

House, it was copied by. Teubner for the second Opera House. The present clock was built by Engineer Ferner from "Spezialwerkstätten für Turm-uhren Meissen" after a small-scale model in the Mathematical and Physical Salon of the Zwinger. It once again occu-pies its original position in the centre of the proscenium. 120 experienced specialists were formed into six "listening groups" for the acoustics tests. Beethoven's "Fidelio" was used for the opera tests; a number of tests were also made for concert performances.

56 The horse-shoe shaped facings of the 1st to 4th balconies determine the form of the auditorium. The segment theme becomes particularly clear in the colonnade of the 5th balcony. The ceiling seems to "float". The underside of the balcony curvatures are decorated with sequences of genii made from photographs by Sigrid Artes and Hans Riedel. The 1st balcony bears medallion reliefs. The reliefs were made by Schulze and Landgraf, they include the soprano Wilhelmine Schröter-Devrient, the tenor Tichatschek, Karoline Neuber and others.

The proscenium is formed by a two-storey column architecture with a surmounted storey borne by caryatids. Both sides are connected by the proscenium frieze. It joins on to the stage portal which is decorated with reliefs and figures of the Muses. The large decorative curtain is framed by an unmovable Harlequin curtain. All folds here are painted as an illusion on a canvas-covered sheet-metal framework. The middle picture depicts "Fantasy with the torch of rapture". She is surrounded by personifications of poetic art and of vocal and instrumental music and by dancers and buffoons.

58 From the aspect of town-planning and architectural design the Elbe bank in the area of Inner Neustadt with the Blockhouse, the Japanese Palais and Grosse Meissner Strasse No. 15 with its double courtyard is of great importance. This historic complex is functionally encompassed by the representative Bellevue Hotel. This burgher house was already mentioned in the town plan in 1632. In 1733, after enlarging by Bähr, it became the Royal Chancellory. Further extended by Exner in 1790 and completed with an attic storey in 1904 this building is the only one of its kind that has remained extant on this bank (the Neustadter) of the river since February 13th, 1945. The new hotel building has 315 rooms and apartments. For the hotel visitors there is a combined banqueting and

conference centre, the "Elbterrasse" Restaurant, the "Palais" Restaurant, the "Buri-Buri" Restaurant and the "Jupiter" Bar. The "Canaletto" Restaurant and the Foyer Bar are to either side of the historic inner courtyard. In the upper storey of the historic building the "Prestige" and "Noblesse" Salons for hotel guests as well as the four salons "Meissen", "Arita", "Moritzburg" and "Pillnitz" are available for small festivities, receptions, etc. In the cellar is "Wackerbarth's Keller" and the "Bierclub No. 15".

The theatre workshops include the costume atelier (2,871 m^2), the scenery painting hall (2,078 m^2) and the workshop building (3,488 m^2). In a palette store still under construction 133 stage sets can be stored at two levels; there are ten boxes for individual props.

missioning of the theatre workshops ahead of schedule in 1982 the State Opera Company officially took over the functional building on June 30th, 1984. Rehearsals and technical trials began in the theatre building on September 6th, 1984.

In all a total of 270 combines, factories and artisan enterprises were under contract to help rebuild the Semper Opera House. Director of Reconstruction, Jeschke, engaged more than 80 artists. On February 13th, 1985, the 40th anniversary of the destruction of the city, the curtain rises for the opening performance. The building workers, architects, engineers and theatre people provide the population of Dresden and their guests from both far and near with testimony to their skills whilst also documenting their desire to maintain our valuable culturo-political heritage and to help this house as well as all its visitors to maintain peace.

Theatre Workshops
of the Semper Opera House Dresden
Ground plan—Ground floor
Costume atelier:
1/2 Entrance
3 Shoemakers' shop
4 Technical centre

Upper storey:
Tailors' shop
Scenery painting hall:
5–7 Paint stores
8 Changing room
9 Scenery painting hall

Upper storey:
Properties painting shop
Workshops building:
12/13 Woodworking shop
14 Machine room
15 Metalworking shop
Upper storey: Turning shop

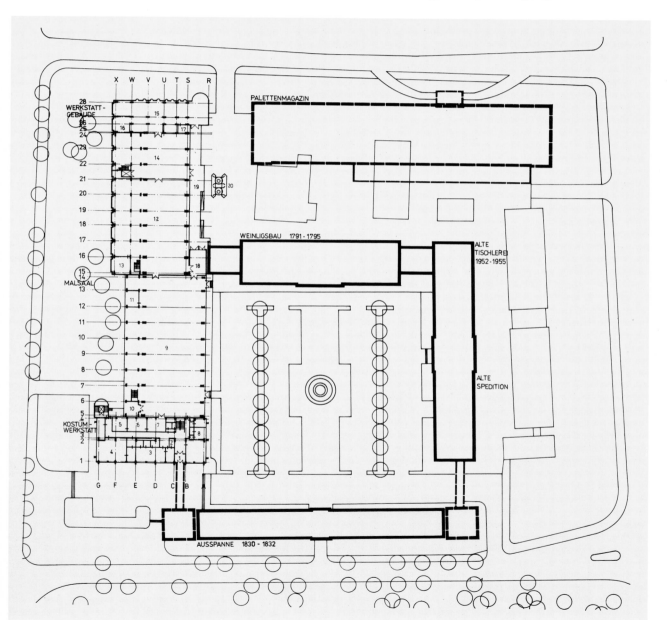

62 The size of the scenery painting hall is coordinated with that of the stage in the theatre building, whereby the dimensions of the cyclorama (50 × 13 metres) were taken into consideration. The painting area (54 × 22 metres) receives shadow-free light through "saw-tooth" roof lights. The hall is 6.3 metres high. A gallery enables the necessary "view from a distance" to be made of the back-drop of the main working stage.

As the exterior architecture indicates rehearsal rooms are built into the centre of the functional building. They receive daylight through skylights; a complementary lighting unit built into the supporting beams can be switched on when necessary. The crystal glass mirrors on its walls and a swinging floor as well as full air conditioning guarantee optimum conditions in the ballet rooms. The rising parquet floor in the choir rehearsal room ensures the choir members a good view of the conductor. The recording studio is situated in the storey below. Project Manager Nürnberger was responsible for this work.

64 The Staatskapelle orchestra has its own rehearsal room situated above the back stage in the theatre building. Walls and ceiling have been specially designed to guarantee the stereoacoustics. The room has been built in such a manner that no sound can reach the stage area. The orchestra seating was manufactured by "VEB Deutsche Werkstätten Hellerau". Acoustic tests carried out by the "Bauakademie der DDR" and Dresden Technical University confirmed that the calculated parameters had been achieved.

Cantilever bridges connect the theatre building with the functional building. The soloists dressing rooms are at the same level as the stage thus ensuring direct accees to the main stage. The dressing rooms for the choir and ballet ensemble are a storey lower. The storey at street level contains management and administrative offices. The rehearsal stage is the same size as the main stage. A view of the sound studio gives an idea of its equipment.

Sound engineer Heischmann from the State Opera Company is working at the control desk.

ENTERPRISES RESPONSIBLE FOR DESIGNING AND BUILDING OPERATIONS

Principal for the Reconstruction:
Reconstruction Management Board of Dresden County Council.
General Contractor and Designer for the Reconstruction of Culturo-Historical Buildings:
VEB (B) Gesellschaftsbau Dresden.
General technical stage design and consultation:
Institut für Kulturbauten Berlin.
Building and stereoacoustic consultation:
Dresden Technical University;
Bauakademie der DDR.
Monument preservation:
Institut für Denkmalpflege, Berlin Arbeitsstelle Dresden.
Visual art and ornamental decoration:
Künstlerkollektiv des Verbandes Bildender Künstler der DDR.
Technical operation concept:
Ingenieurstab der Staatsoper Dresden.
Catering facilities:
Bezirksdirektion des volkseigenen Einzelhandels; Büro für Rationalisierung.
Building work:
VEB (B) Gesellschaftsbau Dresden.
Prefabricated reinforced concrete:
VEB BMK; VEB (B) GBD;
VEB (K) Bau Meissen.
Demolition:
VEB Autobahnkombinat, BT Bohr- und Sprengtechnik.
Structural steelwork for cantilever bridges:
VEB Stahlbau Plauen.
Mobile crane erection:
VEB Industrie Montage Merseburg.
Industrial railway:
Verkehrsbetriebe der Stadt Dresden Industriebahn und Werkstatt Reick.

Steel doors:
Fa. Richter Taubenhein.
Aluminium windows and doors:
VEB Leichtmetallbau Berlin;
VEB Holz- und Leichtbauelemente Leipzig.
Safety glass:
VEB Mehrschichten-Sicherheitsglas Potsdam-Babelsberg.
Timber preservation:
VEB Bautenschutz Freital.
Stage machinery and steel structures:
VEB Sächsischer Brücken- und Stahlhochbau Dresden.
Anchor spindles stage house:
VEB Autobahnbaukombinat, Werkstatt Klotzsche.
Stage lighting:
VEB Kombinat Starkstromanlagenbau Leipzig–Halle.
Hydraulic stage equipment:
VEB Kombinat ORSTA Hydraulik Leipzig.
High voltage equipment:
VEB Elektroanlagen Ostsachsen Zittau; VEB Neon-Müller Dresden;
PGH Elektrobau Nossen.
Lightning potection:
PGH Elektro-Blitz, Dresden.
Low voltage equipment:
VEB Nachrichtenanlagenbau Dresden.
Battery units:
Fa. Kunde Radebeul.
Air-conditioning plant:
VEB Lufttechnische Anlagen Dresden.
Compressors refrigeration machinery:
VEB Maschinenfabrik Halle.
Control-engineering plant:
VEB Geräte- und Reglerwerke Teltow.

Ashlar processing:
VEB Elbenaturstein Dresden.
Stucco artificial marble work:
VEB Ausbau im WBK Dresden.
Stucco Lustrework:
Künstlerkollektiv des Verbandes Bildender Künstler der DDR.
Painting work:
PGH Malerhandwerk Canaletto Dresden.
Sign painting:
PGH Malerhandwerk "Nord" Dresden.
Terrazzo work:
PGH Aufbau Dresden.
Art casting:
VEB Formguss Radeberg; BT Kunstguss Dresden;
VEB Lauchhammerwerk;
VEB Medaillenmünze Dresden.
Fa. Graichen Dresden.
Brass polishing:
VEB Transformatoren- und Röntgenwerk "Hermann Matern" Dresden; Fa. Teche Boxdorf.
Historic lamps:
VEB Spezialleuchtenbau Wurzen.
Special lamps:
VEB Leuchtenbau Radeberg;
Fa. Lahr, Freital.
Engraving:
Fa. Zschiesche Pillnitz.
Lighting glass:
VEB Vereinigte Beleuchtungsglaswerke Dresden.
Models:
Modellwerkstatt des VEB Projektierung Dresden im VEB (B) WBK Dresden.
Patterns:
Fa. Gutschlich Freital.
Special clocks:
Spezialwerkstätten für Turmuhren Meissen.

Radio and communication equipment:
Deutsche Post – Rundfunk- und
Fernsehtechnisches Zentralamt
Berlin.
Passanger and freight lifts:
VEB Sächsischer Brücken- und
Stahlhochbau Dresden;
VEB (B) Heizungs- und Sanitär-
technik Dresden.
Interior decoration:
VEB Innenprojekt Leipzig.
Carpentry and joiners' work:
VEB Deutsche Werkstätten
Hellerau; PGH Bau-Möbel
Bannewitz; Fa. Pohl Pirna;
PGH Bau-Möbel Radeberg.
Concert hall woodwork:
PGH des Tischlerhandwerks
Dresden-Ost.
Large surface mirrors:
VEB Spiegelwerk Wilsdruff.
Theatre chairs:
VEB Forschung und Entwicklung
Rabenau, Betriebsteil Waldheim.
Special wrought-iron work:
Fa. Bergmann Dresden.
Wrought-iron work:
Fa. Heyne Dresden; Fa. Pohl
Dresden; Fa. Beyer Dresden;
Fa. Möbius Saultitz; Fa. Walther
Freital; PGH Landtechnik
Bannewitz; Fa. Portzig Dresden;
Fa. Geburtig Dresden; Fa. Grahl
Wachau; Fa. Klinger-Grossmann
Dresden; Fa. Matschinsky Ruppen-
dorf; Fa. Funke Moritzburg;
Fa. Roch Dresden.
*Flooring, tiling, glazing
and roofing work:*
VEB Ausbau im VEB (B) WBK
Dresden.
Parquetry:
VEB Parkett und Rolladenbau
Halle.

Asphalt work:
PGH Tektas Dresden.
Roof plumbing:
VEB Technische Gebäudeausrü-
stung Dresden;
PGH Moderne Technik Dresden.
Heating and sanitary installations:
VEB (B) Heizungs- und Sanitär-
technik Dresden.
Boiler plant:
VEB Wasserbehandlungsanlagen
Berlin.
Sound absorbing:
VEB Schallisolierung Dresden
im VEB BMK; VEB Raum-
gestaltung und Vlieswerkstoffe
Karl-Marx-Stadt.
Industrial paint:
VEB Korrosionsschutz im
VEB BMK; VEB BMK Großenhain
BT Ausbau; Fa. Angermann
Dresden; VEB Wärme- und Ober-
flächenschutz Dresden.
Galvanising:
VEB Feuerverzinkung Riesa.
Special foundations:
VEB BMK Kohle und Energie
Industriebau Dresden.
Special sealing:
VEB Universal Dresden.
Water pressure sealings:
VEB Spezialbaukombinat Magde-
burg.
*Ground water level sinking
and cooling water supply:*
VEB (B) Verkehrs- und Tiefbau-
kombinat Dresden B 09.
Kitchen equipment:
VEB Handelstechnische Anlagen
Dresden.
Refrigerators:
VEB Kühlanlagenbau Dresden.
*Mechanical civil engineering
and free space work:*

VEB (B) Verkehrs- und Tiefbau-
kombinat Dresden B 02;
VEB (St) Grünanlagenbau Dresden.
Surveying:
VEB Geodäsie und Kartographie
Dresden.
Passementerie:
Fa. Schink Dresden.
Special maintenance scaffolds:
Institut für Leichtbau, Dresden.
Plastic elements:
VEB Plaste Karl-Marx-Stadt.
Sawdust exhaust:
VEB Rationalisierung der Möbel-
industrie Jonsdorf Werk III
Zwenkau.
Transport services:
VEB Kraftverkehr Dresden.
Cleaning:
Dienstleistungskombinat Dresden;
Gottfried-Semper-Club Dresden
beim Kulturbund der DDR
and other bodies and enterprises
who took part in the reconstruction
of the Semper Opera House.
Photo material:
Deutsche Fotothek Dresden;
Institut für Denkmalpflege
Dresden; VEB (B) Gesellschafts-
bau Dresden.

68 Gottfried Semper paid much attention to the design of the stairwells which are also vestibules for two storeys. The public which enters the building from below and from the side has to be guided into the entrance hall in such a manner that the flight of stairs does not break the compact spatial effect of the columned hall in the upper storey. The optical effect of the ceiling picture by Hofmann of the Elbe side and Gonne on the Zwinger side on the lower storey of the respective vestibule as well as the arrangement of the stair flights found Semper's full agreement.

Both vestibules are connected by the Upper Circular Foyer. Semper's concept that colour and material effects should increase from the lower to the upper rooms has been followed and all spatial closing elements have received a more distinguised appearance and festive colour. The arrangement of the columns along the walls varies. The vaulting alternates with a ceiling rich in coffer-work. Wall designs are complemented with bronze candelabras. The central axis is further emphasised by means of a ceiling painting. Here is the entrance to the middle balcony and the exit to the exedra.

70 In the Upper Circular Foyer oval and rectangular pictures alternate. They should "alternate like the jewels on a necklace". The oval pictures are multicoloured; the rectangular, two-coloured and similar to a bronze relief.

The severies of the Upper Vestibule are in light tones contrasting with the red terrazzo floor and a decorated with colourful arabesques. The arches bear repetitive leafwork on a yellow ground. The Lower Circular Foyer is simple and clear in its architecture. The pa-

nelling on the walls consists of richly structured stucco work painted in oak colour.

The ceiling paintings of the vestibule on the Zwinger side depicts Schietzelt's and Symmangk's programme of the thoughts of transfiguration and reconciliation after F. Gonne. "The genius of poetic justice floats over the whole and there follows, in a descending line and in three groups, Lohengrin and Oberon, King Lear and Cordelia, Tamino and Pamina, Knight Templar and Nathan, Maid of Orleans, concluding with Faust and Mephistopheles surrounded by visions." (Steche, R., Der künstlerische Schmuck des neuen Hoftheaters Dresden)

72   In Dresden's townscape there are several constructions connecting historic buildings from various epochs: Palace and Cathedral, Palace and Taschenbergpalais, and now also the Semper Opera House and the functional building. The arrangement of the stone plates in the functional building is continued in the structure of the bridge. Only a few of the sandstone statues were still extant after the fire of 1869 and re-used by Semper. The seated "Moliere" by E. J. Hähnel survived the air raid of 1945.

The idea for the exedra could already be seen in Semper's theatre designs for Rio de Janeiro and Munich. In the preplanning work in 1870 the architect already firmly defined the decoration of the niche with marble inlay work and that of the dome with sculpture and painting. Since its reconstruction the exedra has been a treasure in the "ring" of the foyer. Before its destruction the Semper Opera House was the venue for the premieres of many successful Strauss operas. The "Rosenkavalier" stands as symbol for the responsibility towards Dresden's great music culture and the resurrection of the State Opera Company's own building. (page 74/75)

76   The auditorium, with a width of 26.86 metres and a depth of 24.09 metres, seems small in contrast to the stage are. Many lights are installed in the technical portal and the proscenium box as well as in the 5th balcony, the stage manger's desk behind the portal tower and the control desk for the under and upper stage machinery are the command posts for the technical stage equipment of a modern opera house. The symmetry of the whole building is clearly shown in the axial photo of the big chandelier on page 77.

Every evening, as from the festive opening ceremony on February 13th, 1985—the forthieth anniversary of the destruction of Dresden, many of the city's inhabitants as well as visitors from far and near will direct their steps full of expectation across a festively illuminated Theaterplatz to the Opera House.

In order to retain this beautiful and newly-built cultural centre for the whole of humanity it is necessary to make peace secure.

Verlag Zeit im Bild Dresden
DDR – 8012 Dresden Julian-Grimau-Allee
Text, pages 7–16: Mathias Rank/Horst Seeger
Text, pages 17–80: Klaus Tempel
Photos: Siegfried Thienel
Layout: Alfred Brückner
Printed in the German Democratic Republic
by Grafischer Grossbetrieb Völkerfreundschaft
Dresden
4101-2
001280